Read-About® Geography

# The Mississippi River

### By Allan Fowler

**Consultant**
Linda Cornwell, Learning Resource Consultant,
Indiana Department of Education

Children's Press®
A Division of Grolier Publishing
New York London Hong Kong Sydney
Danbury, Connecticut

Visit Children's Press® on the Internet at:
http://publishing.grolier.com

Designer: Herman Adler Design Group

**Library of Congress Cataloging-in-Publication Data**

Fowler, Allan.
 The Mississippi River / by Allan Fowler.
  p. cm. — (Rookie read-about geography)
 Includes index.
 Summary: Traces the Mississippi River from its source near Canada to the
Gulf of Mexico and discusses its history, towns, and physical features.
 ISBN 0-516-21557-4 (lib. bdg.)          0-516-26556-3 (pbk.)
 1. Mississippi River—Juvenile literature. [1. Mississippi River.]
 I. Titles. II. Series.
 F351.F79    1999                         98-43961
 977—dc21                                 CIP
                                          AC

_C '_

_2/08_

©1999 Children's Press®
A Division of Grolier Publishing Co., Inc.

Lake Itasca

This stream flows out of
Lake Itasca in Minnesota.
If you stand in it, the water
might not reach your knees.
It is the beginning of the
Mississippi River.

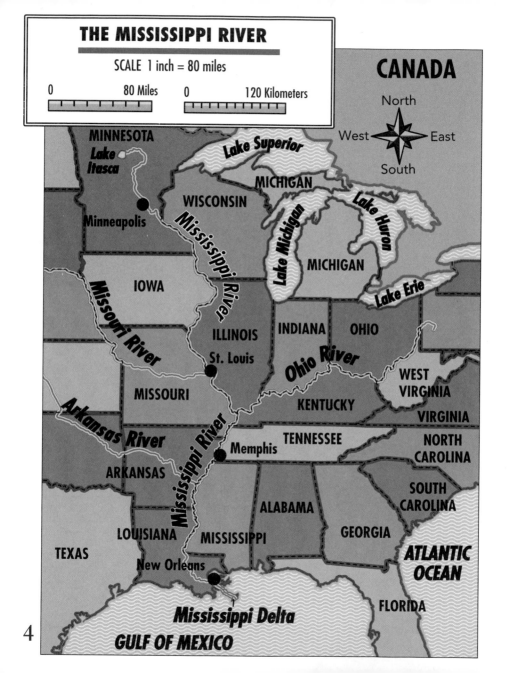

# THE MISSISSIPPI RIVER

SCALE 1 inch = 80 miles

0      80 Miles

0      120 Kilometers

CANADA

North

West   East

South

MINNESOTA

Lake Itasca

Lake Superior

MICHIGAN

WISCONSIN

Lake Michigan

Lake Huron

Minneapolis

Mississippi River

MICHIGAN

Lake Erie

IOWA

Missouri River

INDIANA

OHIO

ILLINOIS

St. Louis

Ohio River

WEST VIRGINIA

MISSOURI

KENTUCKY

VIRGINIA

Arkansas River

Mississippi River

TENNESSEE

Memphis

NORTH CAROLINA

ARKANSAS

SOUTH CAROLINA

ALABAMA

LOUISIANA

MISSISSIPPI

GEORGIA

TEXAS

ATLANTIC OCEAN

New Orleans

FLORIDA

Mississippi Delta

4

GULF OF MEXICO

The river soon becomes wider and deeper.

People call it "the mighty Mississippi." It is 2,340 miles long.

Other rivers flow into the Mississippi and become part of it.

Many cities and towns lie along the Mississippi's banks.

Let's follow the Mississippi as it flows down to the sea.

Fountain City, Wisconsin, along the Mississippi River

At Minneapolis, Minnesota, the river spills over the Falls of St. Anthony.

Falls of St. Anthony

Barges in the Mississippi

No boats can go past them.
Below the falls, barges carry
goods to and from cities.

A barge is a boat with a flat bottom. It has no sails or engine.

It must be pulled or pushed along by a towboat.

One small towboat can move a long row of barges.

People used to travel
along the Mississippi
on riverboats.

That was before there
were planes and cars.

A few riverboats, such
as the *Delta Queen,*
still carry people.

*Delta Queen* riverboat

Missouri River        confluence        Mississippi River

Confluence of the Missouri and the Mississippi rivers

The Missouri River joins
the Mississippi near the
city of St. Louis, Missouri.

The place where two
rivers meet is called a
"confluence."

The Gateway Arch stands next to the Mississippi in St. Louis.

Further south, the Ohio River joins the Mississippi.

Later, the Arkansas River joins it.

Gateway Arch

Farm buildings under floodwaters

In the spring, ice and snow melt. The melted water flows into the rivers, and makes them rise.

Rivers sometimes spill over their banks. The water can cover farms and towns.

This is called a flood.

Levees (LEV-eez) have been built along the Mississippi.

Levees are walls or mounds. Many are made of earth.

They keep the river from flowing over its banks.

A levee made with earth-filled bags

The Mississippi passes other cities, such as Memphis, Tennessee, and New Orleans, Louisiana.

New Orleans, Louisiana

Memphis, Tennessee

A Louisiana bayou

24

Below New Orleans, the river spreads out into swamps called bayous (BYE-ooz).

The Mississippi carries a lot of soil and bits of rock called "silt."

The silt builds up at the end of the river. It forms new land called a delta.

Silt in river water

Mississippi River

Land

Delta

Gulf of Mexico

View of the Mississippi Delta from the air

The Mississippi River ends at its delta.

The water then pours into the Gulf of Mexico.

# Words You Know

barges

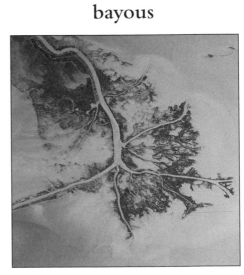

bayous

confluence

delta

falls

flood

Gateway Arch

levees

riverboats

silt

stream

towboat

31

# Index

# About the Author

Allan Fowler is a freelance writer with a background in advertising.
Born in New York, he lives in Chicago now and enjoys traveling.

# Photo Credits

Photographs ©: Gamma-Liaison: 7 (Larry Mayer), 21, 31 middle left (Jeff
Topping); H. Armstrong Roberts, Inc.: cover (H. Abernathy), 23 (W. Bertsch),
9 (J. Blank) : 10, 30 top left, 31 bottom right (R. Kord); Landslides Aerial
Photography: 14, 30 bottom left (Alex S. MacLean); NASA: 28, 30 bottom right;
New England Stock Photo: 17, 31 top right (John C. Whyte); Photo
Researchers: 13, 31 middle center (Paolo Koch); Superstock, Inc.: 8, 31 top left;
Tony Stone Images: 18, 31 top center (Cameron Davidson); Viesti Collection,
Inc.: 22 (Gauvin); Visuals Unlimited: 24, 30 top right (Bruce Berg), 3, 31 bottom
left (Scott Berner), 27, 31 middle right (Ted Whittenkraus).
Map by Joe LeMonnier.